T0022968

To Mirte, Seppe, and Hanne,
who help me rediscover the world every single day.
– *Jan Leyssens*

Copyright © 2022 Clavis Publishing Inc., New York

Originally published as *Wonderwaar. Tocht naar de Noordpool*
in Belgium and the Netherlands by Clavis Uitgeverij, 2021
English translation from the Dutch by Clavis Publishing Inc., New York

Visit us on the Web at www.clavis-publishing.com.

No part of this publication may be reproduced or stored in a retrieval system,
or transmitted in any form or by any means, electronic, mechanical, photocopying,
recording, or otherwise, without the prior written permission of the publisher,
except in the case of brief quotations embodied in critical articles and reviews.
For information regarding permissions, write to Clavis Publishing, info-US@clavisbooks.com.

Airship to the Arctic written by Jan Leyssens and illustrated by Joachim Sneyers

ISBN 978-1-60537-740-7

This book was printed in November 2021 at Nikara, M. R. Štefánika 858/25, 963 01 Krupina, Slovakia.

First Edition
10 9 8 7 6 5 4 3 2 1

Clavis Publishing supports the First Amendment and celebrates the right to read.

AIRSHIP
TO THE
ARCTIC

Written by Jan Leyssens
Illustrated by Joachim Sneyers

Clavis

NEW YORK

In China, sky lanterns were probably used as early as 1800 years ago to light up the sky at night during wars. But the first hot air balloon wasn't released until 300 years ago. It all started in Portugal.

Bartolomeu Lourenço de Gusmão was a Brazilian-Portuguese priest who wanted to build the very first airship ever for the Portuguese king. To convince the king that he was capable of making such a ship fly, Bartolomeu filled a paper balloon with hot air. He let it fly to the ceiling of the palace.

The king was so impressed that he immediately made Bartolomeu a professor at the university and appointed him one of the most important scientists of the kingdom.

The first *real* hot air balloons were developed in the summer of 1783 in France. In June of that year, the Montgolfier brothers presented the first hot air balloon with a basket to a large audience. They did so at the royal palace of Versailles. Because no one knew whether people could survive at high altitudes, later three animals were chosen as passengers for a test flight: a duck, a rooster, and a sheep. It was thought that the sheep's body would be somewhat similar to a human's. The sheep was even given a name: Montauciel, which is French for "ascend to heaven." The animals returned safe and sound and went down in history as the very first balloonists.

In August, the Robert brothers made the very first balloon filled with hydrogen, a flammable gas that's released when you combine an acid and metal. The balloon flew more than 20 kilometers (12 miles) and landed in the meadow of a farmer in a small village. The villagers were so frightened by the strange object that they attacked it with pitchforks and clubs.

Over the next few months, many more balloons were designed and tested. In November, the first people flew a hot air balloon. A month later, the first manned hydrogen balloon flight took place.

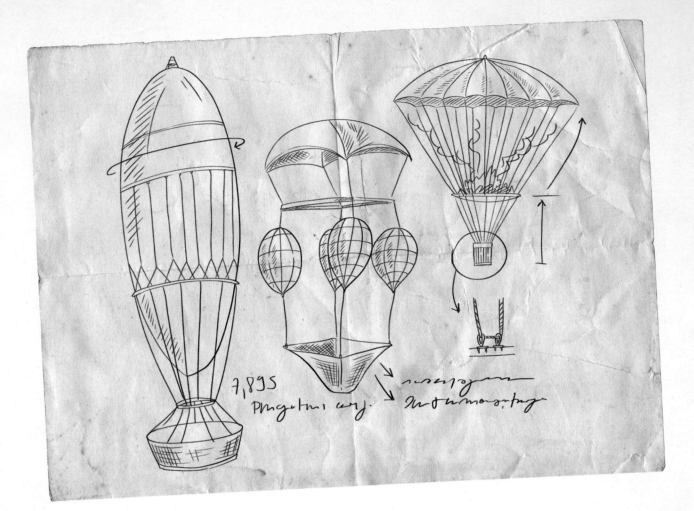

During the subsequent years, many new balloons and balloon flights followed. One challenge soon became clear: you can't really steer a balloon. Either you depend on the wind or the balloon is held in place by a cord.

Many scientists and engineers began to think about how to put propellers and steering wheels on the balloons to create airships that they could control.

In 1852, almost 100 years after the first balloon flights, Frenchman Henri Giffard managed to make a controlled flight with an airship. The hydrogen balloon was powered by a steam engine, which made a propeller spin to steer the balloon. Henri flew 27 kilometers (17 miles) over Paris, showing spectators how he steered his vessel, the Giffard dirigible (or "steerable Giffard"), in all sorts of directions.

After Henri's successful flight, many other airships were built. You may have heard of the airships called *Zeppelins*. Designed by Ferdinand von Zeppelin, they became popular in the early 1900s. Sadly, the most famous of these was the *Hindenburg*, which tragically exploded in 1937.

In 1897, Roald Amundsen didn't travel by airship, but with a seagoing vessel. Roald was a Norwegian explorer who researched the polar regions.

In that year, he sailed along as second mate on a Belgian Antarctic expedition. The plan was to further map the Antarctic. The ship, the *Belgica*, became the first vessel to spend the winter in Antarctica after getting trapped in the pack ice.

A few years later, one of his colleagues claimed to have reached the North Pole, the northernmost point of the Earth at the Arctic. And so in 1911, Roald went on a new expedition to Antarctica to become the first person ever to go to the South Pole, the southernmost point of the Earth at the Antarctic. When he reached the pole on December 14 after a long journey, he and his travel companions camped there for three days. By means of measurements of the stars, he wanted to make sure that he had reached the tip of the pole.

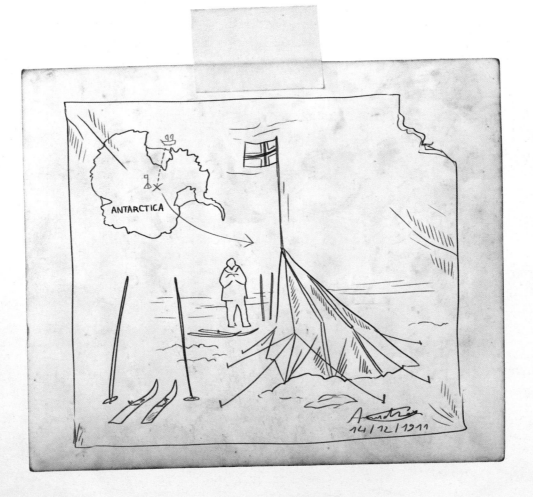

Because more and more people began to doubt whether the North Pole had really been reached, Roald began to make his own attempts. In 1925, he and American explorer Lincoln Ellsworth attempted to get there by plane. Due to strong winds, they landed far from the real pole. When they wanted to fly home again, it ultimately took Roald and Lincoln almost an entire month to make a runway in the ice.

Umberto Nobile

After that attempt, Roald thought that it might be more interesting to fly over the pole with an airship that didn't have to land on the ice. He contacted the Italian airship engineer and pilot Umberto Nobile. Umberto was willing to design a special airship on the condition that he would be captain and that five Italian crew members would accompany him.

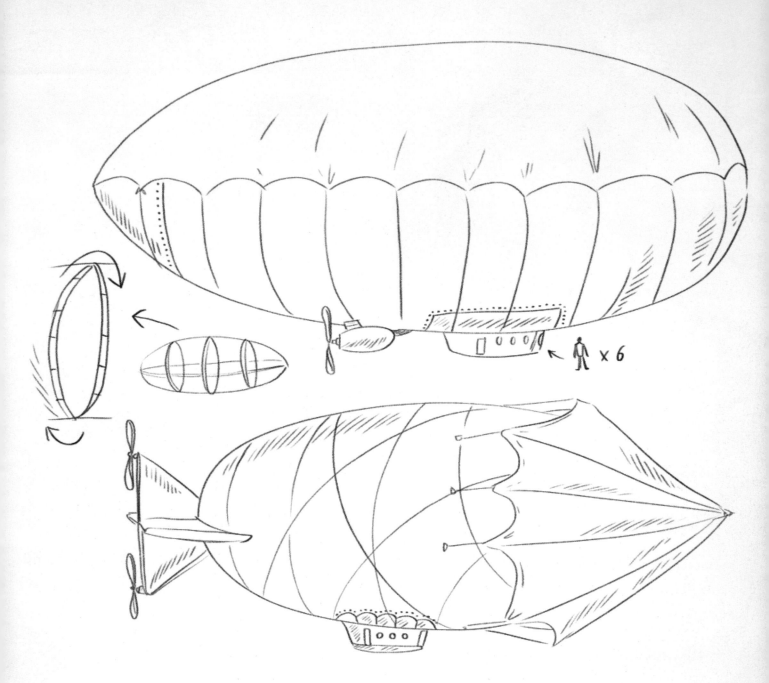

U mberto's biggest challenge was to build the airship so that it could with-
stand the harsh weather conditions over the Arctic. After some modifi-
cations, the airship was handed over to the flying club of Norway in a grand
ceremony. The club paid for most of the expedition. The ship was named *Norge*
and was flown from Rome to Oslo in the next few days.

To reach the North Pole, Roald had figured out that they could first fly up to the northernmost town in Norway. There, they could stock up on additional supplies and make the final adjustments to the ship. On May 5, 1926, they left for the North Pole. Seven days later, on May 12, the group reached the pole. On a rope, they lowered a Norwegian, an Italian, and an American flag.

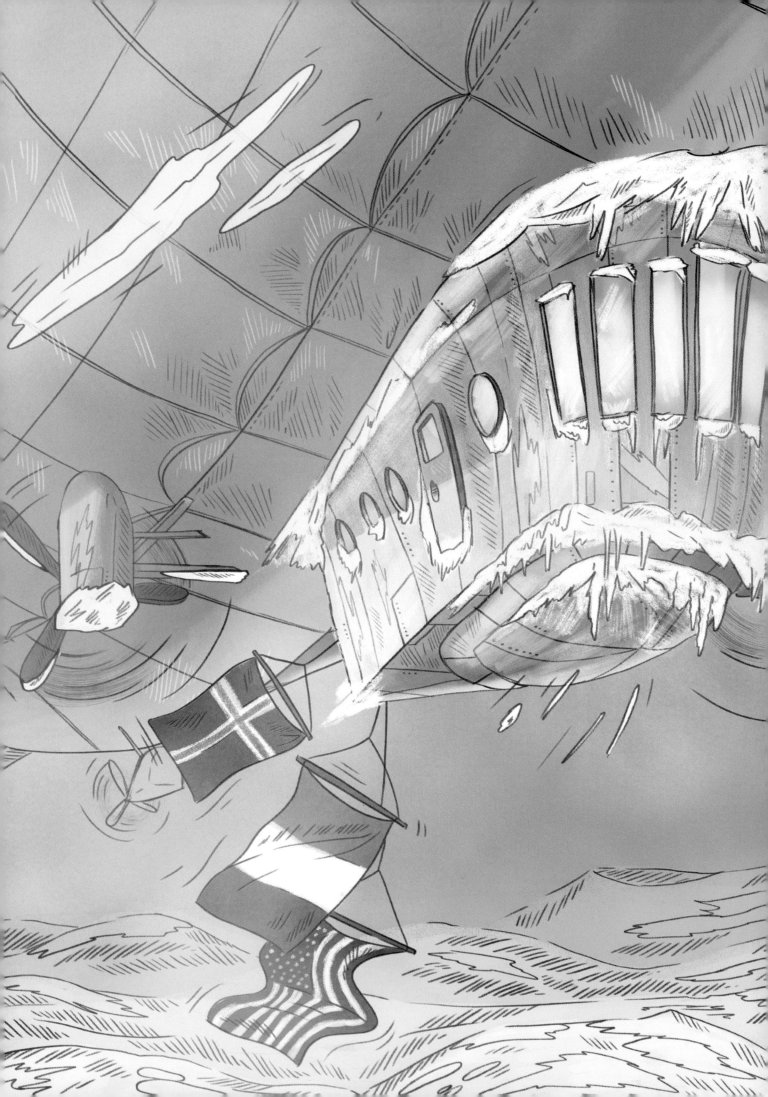

The expedition certainly wasn't without dangers. Shortly after they reached the North Pole, a dense fog surrounded the *Norge*, which froze to the ship like ice due to the cold. Ice also coated the propeller. The pieces of ice shot at the balloon like knives, so the crew had to keep repairing the balloon canvas. But the repair materials were running out. Roald and Umberto had to try to reach a village or town as quickly as possible. The bad weather kept blowing them back and forth, but after nearly 72 hours, they finally reached a small village in Alaska.

1926 - Alaska

X3

After they recovered a bit from their adventure, the crew traveled back to Norway by boat. There, a large group of people was waiting for them. Not only were they the first to ever reach the North Pole, the *Norge* was also the very first airship to fly from the European continent to North America. Various aircraft still use the route today.

And so, with the help of an airship, Roald Amundsen was the first person ever to reach both the South Pole and the North Pole.

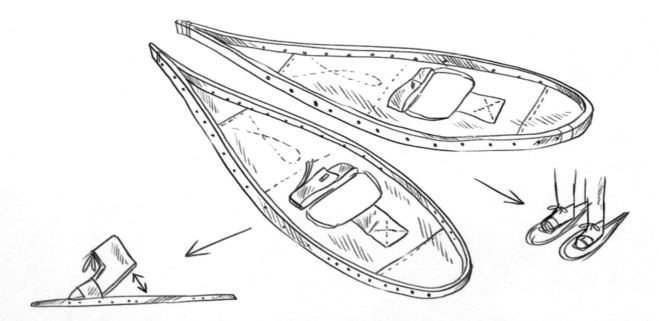

From 1920 onwards, airships were quickly overtaken by airplanes to fly from one place to another. Many of the gases in the balloons were also very dangerous: they could explode.

In recent years, however, many aircraft manufacturers are rediscovering the airship. It's a very sustainable way of making flights that can take a little longer. Airships can be used to transport products, as many seagoing vessels do now, but also to make long air cruises along the least accessible places on our planet.

There are even ideas of using airships in space. On gas planets like Venus, we could build entire flying cities in the future . . . The possibilities are endless!

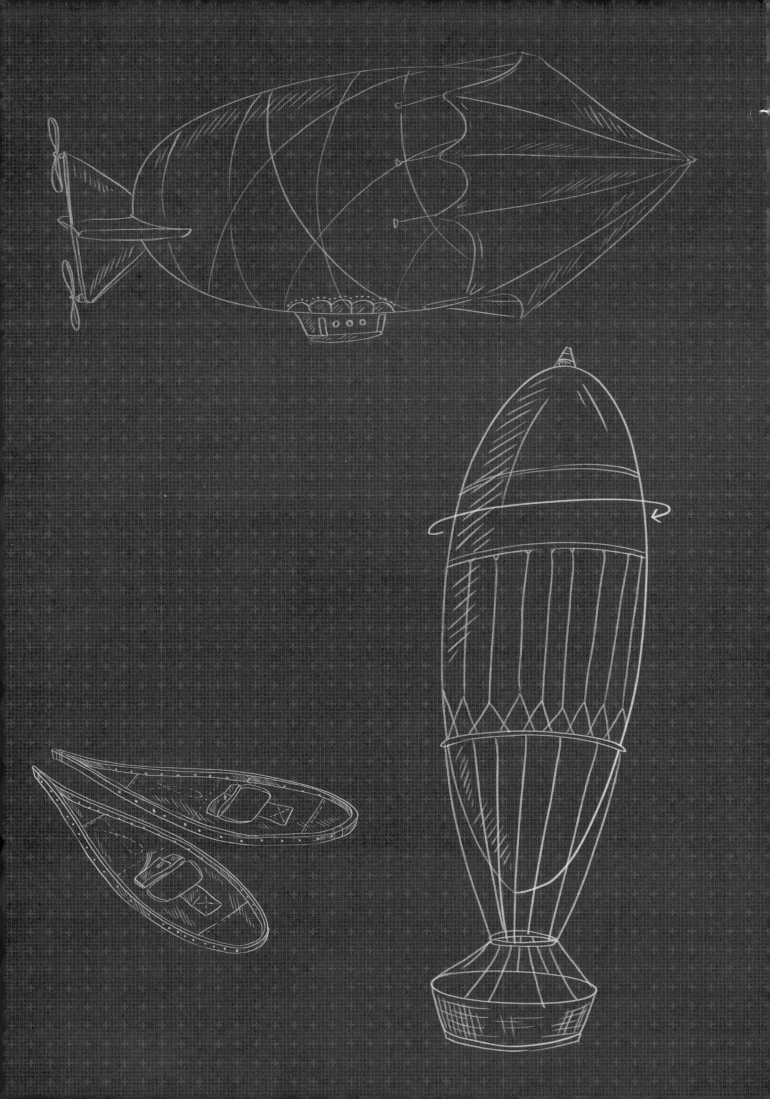